Contents

Animal body parts

Animals have different body parts.

spines

Some animals have spines.

What are spines?

Spines are spiky body parts.

Some spines are made of bone.

Some spines are made of hard hairs.

Different spines

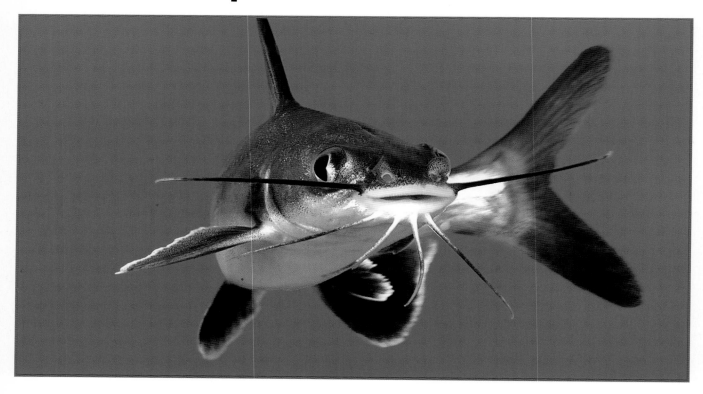

Spines grow on different parts of animals' bodies.

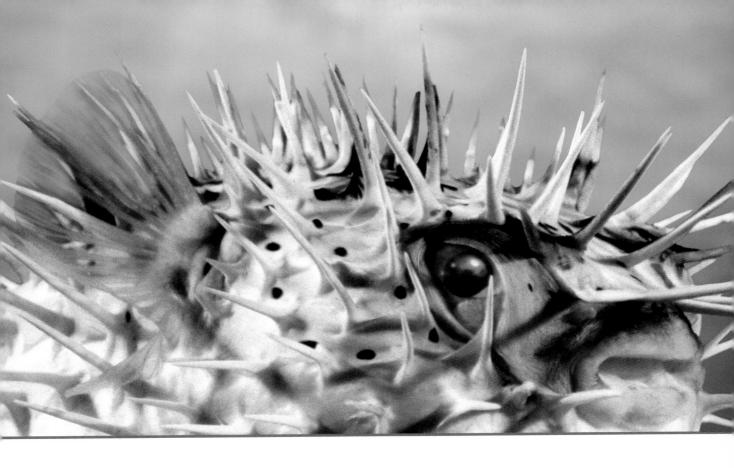

Some spines are short.
What animal is this?

This animal is a porcupine fish. Its spines tell animals not to eat it!

Some spines are colourful.
What animal is this?

This animal is a sea urchin.

Its spines tell fish to stay away.

Some spines are brown and white.
What animal is this?

This animal is a hedgehog. It rolls into a spiny ball to keep safe.

Some spines are long and webbed.
What animal is this?

sail

This animal is a sailfish. Its spines hold up its tall sail.

Some spines are in long rows.
What animal is this?

This animal is an iguana. Its spines help to scare other animals away.

Your body

Do you have spines?

No! You do not have spines.

Humans grow skin and hair on their bodies.

Can you remember?

Which animal rolls into a spiny ball to keep safe?

Picture glossary

spines sharp, pointed body parts that grow on an animal's body

webbed joined together by skin. Webbed feet have skin that joins the toes together.

Index

Notes for parents and teachers

Before reading

Show children the front cover of the book. Guide children in a discussion about what they think the book will be about. Tell children that spines are spiky body parts on animals. Can they think of animals that have spines? Then, discuss that spines are body parts and are used for different things.

After reading

Give out pictures of animals with spines (cut from magazines or printed from the internet). Ask the children to sort out animals with spines who live in the ocean from animals with spines who live on land. Help the children to create collages showing the variety of animals in each group. Encourage the children to compare the animals and to discuss the similarities and differences they find with a partner.